seems like
scrappy

JUL   2015

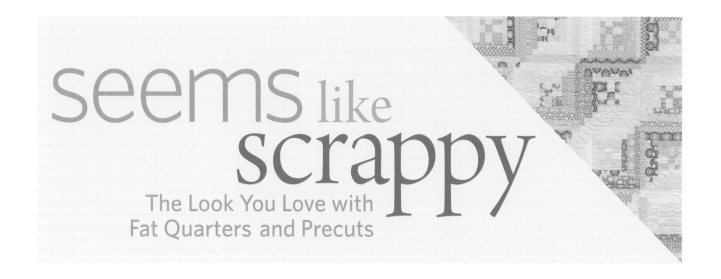

seems like scrappy

The Look You Love with Fat Quarters and Precuts

Rebecca Silbaugh

Martingale
Create with Confidence

Dedication

To my Duncan Christopher, the best quilting dog a girl could ask for.

Seems Like Scrappy: The Look You Love with Fat Quarters and Precuts
© 2015 by Rebecca Silbaugh

Martingale®
19021 120th Ave. NE, Ste. 102
Bothell, WA 98011-9511 USA
ShopMartingale.com

Printed in China
20 19 18 17 16 15   8 7 6 5 4 3 2 1

Library of Congress Cataloging-in-Publication Data is available upon request.

ISBN: 978-1-60468-585-5

Mission Statement

Dedicated to providing quality products and service to inspire creativity.

Credits

PUBLISHER AND CHIEF VISIONARY OFFICER
Jennifer Erbe Keltner

EDITORIAL DIRECTOR
Karen Costello Soltys

DESIGN DIRECTOR
Paula Schlosser

ACQUISITIONS EDITOR
Karen M. Burns

PHOTOGRAPHER
Brent Kane

TECHNICAL EDITOR
Nancy Mahoney

PRODUCTION MANAGER
Regina Girard

COPY EDITOR
Tiffany Mottet

COVER AND INTERIOR DESIGNER
Connor Chin

ILLUSTRATOR
Christine Erikson

Contents

Introduction

I don't think it's a secret that I love scrappy quilts and it's apparent many of you do too! I'm super excited to be back with another collection of scrappy quilts using my seamingly scrappy method, where I use precuts and fabric bundles to mimic the look of scrap quilts without the need for a stash.

There is a definite charm about scrap quilts, especially quilts with stories. Many antique quilts and heirloom treasures were made in a time where quilts were more for function than fashion. It's fun to look at these quilts and know that their makers didn't have an endless amount of fabric available through local shops or the Internet. Many quilts were made with pieces of worn-out clothing, older quilts that had seen better days, and a small selection of new fabrics. Yet, with the limits set before them, those quilters made gorgeous quilts with tons of personality using what was available.

Thinking back on this history, I realize that we quilters are so spoiled nowadays. If I want to order a charm pack from an online shop at three in the morning and have it show up at my door a few days later, with a click of the mouse, it's done. How awesome is that?

This collection of quilts is my personal tribute to the scrappy quilts of yesteryear, and it can be yours too! And the best part is you don't need a stash and an endless pile of little pieces to choose from. Using inspiration from traditional quilts of the past, the precut fabrics available now, and a little ingenuity, I came up with these patterns to share with you.

Precuts Abound!

Here are some of the commonly available precut packages that I've used to make the quilts in this book:

Charm packs: 40 assorted 5" squares*

Layer Cakes: 40 assorted 10" squares (available from Moda)

Jelly Rolls and Tonga Treats: 40 assorted 2½"-wide strips (available from Moda and Timeless Treasures, respectively)

Tonga Treats 6-pack: 20 assorted 6"-wide strips (available from Timeless Treasures)

Honeycombs: 40 assorted 6" hexagons (available from Moda)

Fat quarters: 18" x 21" cuts of fabric, available individually or in bundles

Fat eighths: 9" x 21" cuts of fabric, available individually or in bundles

Your charm pack may contain more or less than 40 squares. Be sure to check!

Most of the quilts in this book have a traditional undertone, but there are a few modern ones mixed in, so I'm sure you'll find something to fall in love with. Plus, I've sprinkled tips and tricks throughout the book to help you achieve the scrappy look you love. You won't believe how easy and fun it can be until you try. Without further ado, it's time for the quilts!

~ Rebecca Silbaugh

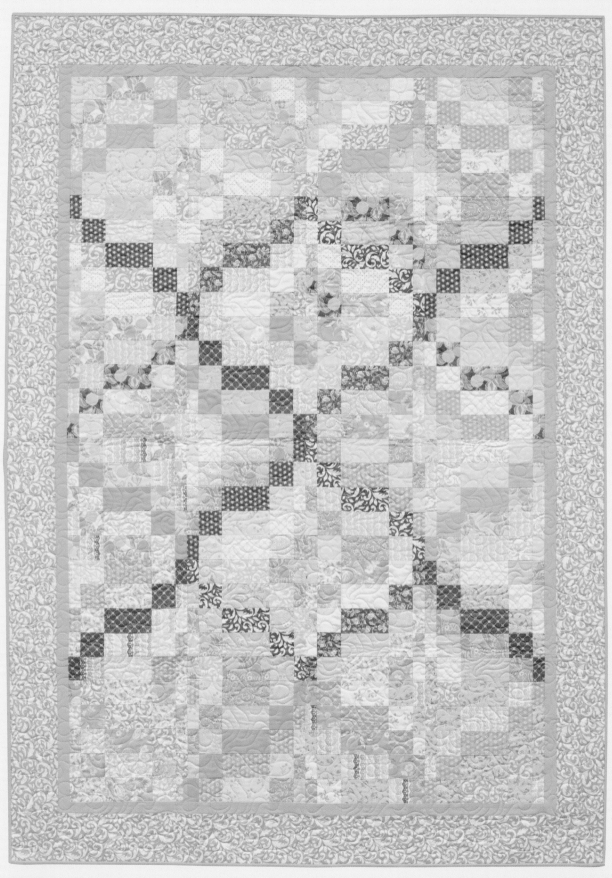

"Wayfarer"
Finished quilt: 50½" x 70½"
Finished block: 10" x 10"

Wayfarer

Blending favorite aspects of a Trip around the World quilt and the styling of a Bargello quilt creates a unique design. Originally I had the name "Trip on a Barge" in mind for this quilt, but it didn't sound as elegant as the quilt looked. Whatever you call it, the design offers plenty of movement.

Materials

Yardage is based on 42"-wide fabric.

1 Jelly Roll *OR* 40 strips, 2½" x 42", of assorted prints for blocks

1 yard of green print for outer border

⅓ yard of pink dot for inner border

⅝ yard of fabric for binding

3½ yards of fabric for backing

58" x 78" piece of batting

SCRAPPY TIP

Fabric Selection

For this quilt, a mix of light, medium, and dark prints works best. You want good contrast between the prints so the bargello design doesn't become lost.

Cutting

From *each* assorted print strip, cut:
3 strips, 2½" x 14" (120 total)

From the pink dot, cut:
6 strips, 1½" x 42"

From the green print, cut:
7 strips, 4½" x 42"

From the fabric for binding, cut:
7 strips, 2¼" x 42"

Making the Blocks

1. Randomly select five print 2½" x 14" strips and lay them out as shown, making sure to have good contrast between each strip. Place the boldest or darkest strip at the bottom of the grouping. Make sure there is good contrast between the top and bottom strips as well.

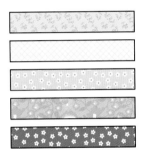

2. Sew the five strips together in order to make a strip set. Press the seam allowances in the directions indicated. Repeat to make a total of 24 strip sets.

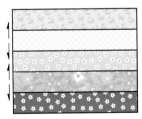

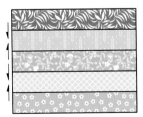

Make 12 of each.

Dark vs. Bold

Sometimes it's hard to distinguish the bold fabrics in a collection based on the principles of light, medium, and dark. This is where value and saturation come into play. Squint your eyes and look at a group of fabrics; it's much easier to see which fabric is the boldest. It may be a red or a bright color, or it may be the odd color that doesn't seem to belong to the group. Don't always assume that darker means bolder. Squinting also allows you to see color instead of pattern, which focuses your brain on the true value of the fabrics. It looks goofy, but it works, give it a try!

3. Choose 12 strip sets to be A or "up" blocks and 12 to be B or "down" blocks. On each strip set for block A, fold the boldest strip up to match the raw edge of the top strip, right sides together. Stitch along the raw edges to create a tube. Make 12 tubes. Set aside the remaining strip sets for the B blocks.

Make 12.

4. Cut each tube across the seam lines, in the order listed, to create the following segments: 1½", 2½", 4½", 2½", and 1½" wide.

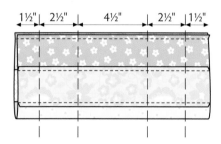

5. Starting with the first 1½"-wide section, remove the line of stitching that created the tube. On the first 2½"-wide section, with the stitching that created the tube at the top and working in a counterclockwise direction, remove the next row of stitching. Continuing around the tube in a counterclockwise direction, remove the seam in each of the remaining sections as shown. Keep the five sections in order while you work.

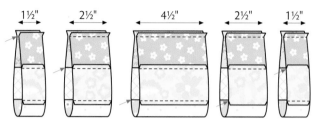

Remove seams indicated by red arrows.

6. Once all of the sections are flat, carefully clip the seam allowances of the seam that created the tube (unless the stitching has already been removed), making sure to clip up to, but not through, the stitching. Press the seam allowances in alternating directions as shown. This will help nest the seams when constructing the block later. Again, keep the five sections in order while you work.

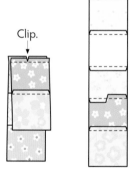

Clip.

Press.

7. Sew the sections together to make a block. Press the seam allowances away from the center of the block. Repeat to make a total of 12 A blocks.

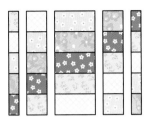

Block A.
Make 12.

8. To create the tube for the B blocks, position the strip set so the boldest strip is at the top. Fold the bottom strip up to meet the raw edge of the boldest strip, right sides together, and stitch the edges together. Make 12 tubes.

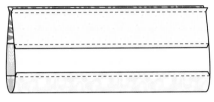

Make 12.

9. Repeat step 4 to cut each tube into sections. Repeat step 5, removing the stitching that created the tube in the first section. Then, working around the sections in a clockwise direction, remove the stitching in each of the remaining sections as shown. Keep the five sections in order while you work.

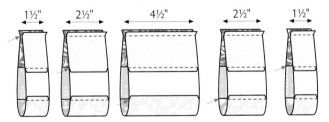

Remove seams indicatated by red arrows.

10. Once all of the sections are flat, carefully clip the seam allowances of the seam that created the tube (unless the stitching has already been removed). Press the seam allowances in alternating directions as shown. Remember to keep the five sections in order as you work.

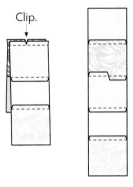

Press.

11. Sew the sections together to make a block. Press the seam allowances toward the center of the block. Make a total of 12 B blocks.

Block B.
Make 12.

Assembling the Quilt Top

1. Lay out the A and B blocks in six rows of four blocks each, alternating them as shown in the quilt assembly diagram on page 12 to mimic a Trip around the World setting. Sew the blocks together in rows. Press the seam allowances in opposite directions from row to row, and then sew the rows together. Press the seam allowances in one direction.

2. Measure the width of the quilt top through the middle and near both edges; determine the average of these measurements. Trim two of the pink-dot strips to the average width. Sew the strips to the top and the bottom of the quilt, matching the ends and easing in any excess. Press the seam allowances toward the border strips.

3. Join the remaining pink-dot strips end to end. Measure the length of the quilt top through the middle and near both edges; determine the average of these measurements. From the pieced strip, cut two strips to the average length. Sew the strips to the sides of the quilt, matching the ends and easing in any excess. Press the seam allowances toward the border strips.

4. For the outer border, join the green-print strips end to end. Repeat steps 2 and 3 to sew the green strips to the quilt top, starting with the sides, and then adding the top and bottom borders.

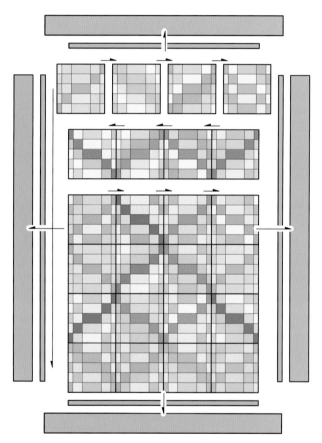

Quilt assembly

Finishing the Quilt

For more information on layering, quilting, or binding, go to ShopMartingale.com/HowtoQuilt and download free illustrated information.

1. Cut and piece the backing fabric so it measures 6" to 8" larger than the quilt top in both directions.

2. Quilt as desired. Quilts with plenty of movement, like this one, have many options when it comes to quilting. You can play up the bold lines with a custom design or let the quilt speak for itself by downplaying the quilting to add texture without taking away from the quilt design. I chose to add texture to this quilt with a floral design.

3. Use the 2¼"-wide binding strips to bind the quilt.

Splotch

This small quilt uses a fairly new precut shape called a Honeycomb, which is a hexagon. This block is made simply, but packs a punch of character, showcasing your fabrics in a unique setting.

Materials

Yardage is based on 42"-wide fabric.

1½ yards of gray dot for blocks and borders

1 Honeycomb OR 36 hexagons (6") of assorted solids for blocks*

⅓ yard of fabric for binding

1¼ yards of fabric for backing

43" x 43" piece of batting

Template plastic**

60° ruler (optional)**

Each Honeycomb hexagon measures 6" from point to opposite point, and 5¼" from one flat side to the opposite side. Or, use the hexagon pattern on page 17 to cut your own hexagons.

**Template plastic is not required if using a ruler. The ruler needs to have a vertical center line and measurements along the horizontal lines, not side measurements.*

Cutting

From *each* assorted solid hexagon, cut:
   4 equal quarters (144 total)*

From the gray dot, cut:
   6 strips, 3" x 42"; crosscut into 72 squares, 3" x 3"
   1 strip, 5" x 42"; crosscut into 36 rectangles, 1" x 5"
   4 strips, 1½" x 42"; crosscut into:
      6 rectangles, 1½" x 9½"
      2 strips, 1½" x 29½"
   4 strips, 3½" x 42"

From the fabric for binding, cut:
   4 strips, 2¼" x 42"

Refer to cutting guide, above right.

Fold the hexagon in half vertically to make a crease. Cut along the crease. Then cut the hexagon in half horizontally from point to point.

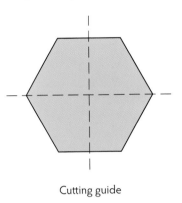

Cutting guide

Making the Blocks

1. Randomly select two quarter hexagons and stitch them together, creating a half-block unit. Press the seam allowances to the right. Make 72 units.

Make 72.

2. Randomly select two units from step 1 and sew them together, nesting the vertical seams. Carefully clip the seam allowances in the center of the block. Clip up to, *but not through*, the stitching. Press the seam allowances in the directions shown. *Do not* trim the dog-ears from the blocks. Make 36 pieced hexagons.

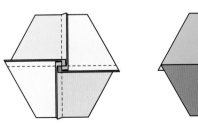

Make 36.

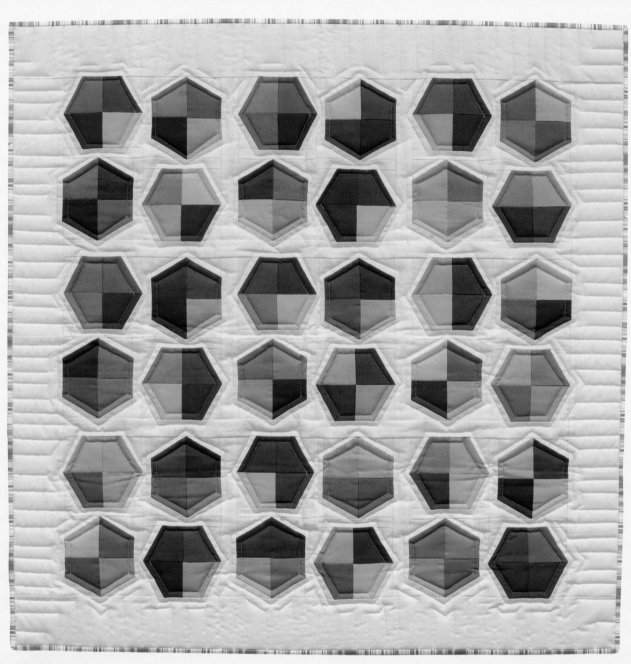

"Splotch"
Finished quilt: 35½" x 35½"
Finished block: 4½" x 4½"

3. Use the triangle pattern on page 17 to make a template. Use the template (or a 60° ruler) to cut 36 of the gray-dot 3" squares in half as follows. Place each square *right side up* on a cutting mat. Align the triangle template with the edges of the square. (If using a 60° ruler, align the vertical centerline along the left side of each square and the 4" line on the ruler along the bottom of the square.) Use a rotary cutter to cut along the right edge of the template or ruler to make a total of 72 triangles. Place the remaining 36 gray-dot squares *wrong side up* on a cutting mat and cut the squares in half in the same way as before to make 72 reversed triangles.

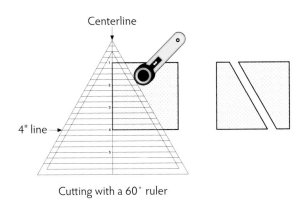

Cutting with a 60° ruler

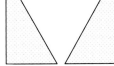

Make 72 of each.

4. Place a gray-dot reversed triangle on the bottom-right corner of a pieced hexagon, right sides together and raw edges aligned. The narrow edge of the triangle should be aligned with the dog ear on the hexagon. There should be excess gray fabric on both sides of the hexagon. Stitch and press the seam allowances toward the gray triangle. In the same way, sew a reversed gray triangle to the

top-left corner of the pieced hexagon. Trim the excess gray fabric even with the edges of the hexagon as shown. Make a total of 36 units.

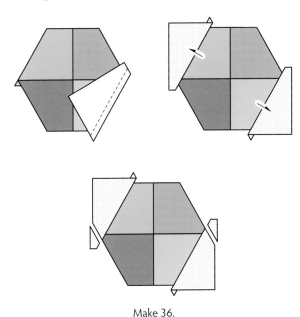

Make 36.

5. Place a gray triangle on the bottom-left corner of a unit from step 4, right sides together and raw edges aligned. Make sure the triangle extends at least ¼" beyond the hexagon, so that you have excess fabric on both sides of the hexagon. Stitch and press the seam allowances toward the triangle. In the same way sew a gray triangle to the top-right corner of the hexagon. Press the seam allowances toward the triangle. Make 36.

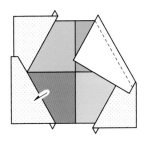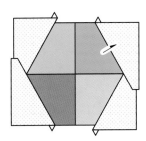

Make 36.

6. Trim the top and bottom edges of the triangles even with the pieced hexagon. Trim each side edge, making sure to leave ¼" beyond the point of each side seam. Stitch a gray-dot 1" x 5" rectangle to the top of the unit to complete a block. Press the seam allowances toward the rectangle. Make a total of 36 blocks.

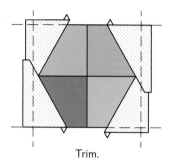

Trim.

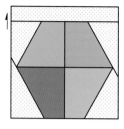

Make 36.

Assembling the Quilt Top

1. Randomly select two blocks, rotate one 90° as shown, and stitch the blocks together. Press the seam allowances in the directions indicated. Make 18 half-block units. Sew two units together to make nine large blocks.

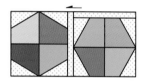

Make 18.

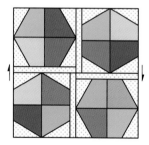

Make 9.

2. Lay out the large blocks and gray-dot 1½" x 9½" strips in three rows as shown in the quilt assembly diagram at right. Sew the blocks and strips in each row together. Press the seam allowances toward the gray-dot strips. Each row should measure 29½" long.

3. Alternately sew the block rows and gray-dot 1½" x 29½" strips together, beginning and ending with a block row. Press the seam allowances toward the gray-dot strips.

4. Measure the length of the quilt top through the middle and near both edges; determine the average of these measurements. Trim two of the gray-dot 3½"-wide strips to the average length. Sew these strips to the sides of the quilt, matching the ends and easing in any excess. Press the seam allowances toward the border strips.

5. Measure the width of the quilt top through the middle and near both edges; determine the average of these measurements. Trim the two remaining gray-dot 3½"-wide strips to the average width. Sew these strips to the top and bottom of the quilt, matching the ends and easing in any excess. Press the seam allowances toward the border strips.

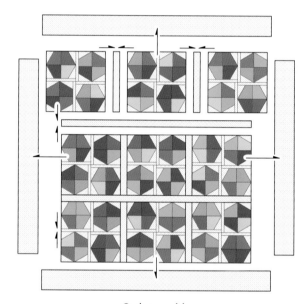

Quilt assembly

SCRAPPY TIP

Fashion Outlaws

Instead of solids, why not try using fabrics you wouldn't normally pair together. Plaids with paisleys? Sure! Florals and stripes? Go for it! Throw out all of the fashion rules about what not to pair together when selecting quilting fabrics. Remember, there are no rules in quilting.

Finishing the Quilt

For more information on layering, quilting, or binding, go to ShopMartingale.com/HowtoQuilt and download free illustrated information.

1. Cut the backing fabric so it measures 6" to 8" larger than the quilt top in both directions.

2. Quilt as desired. A quilt like this one lends itself nicely to sharp angles and modern designs, but can easily be softened with bubbles and swirls too. I outline quilted around the hexagons and filled in the border with straight lines.

3. Use the 2¼"-wide binding strips to bind the quilt.

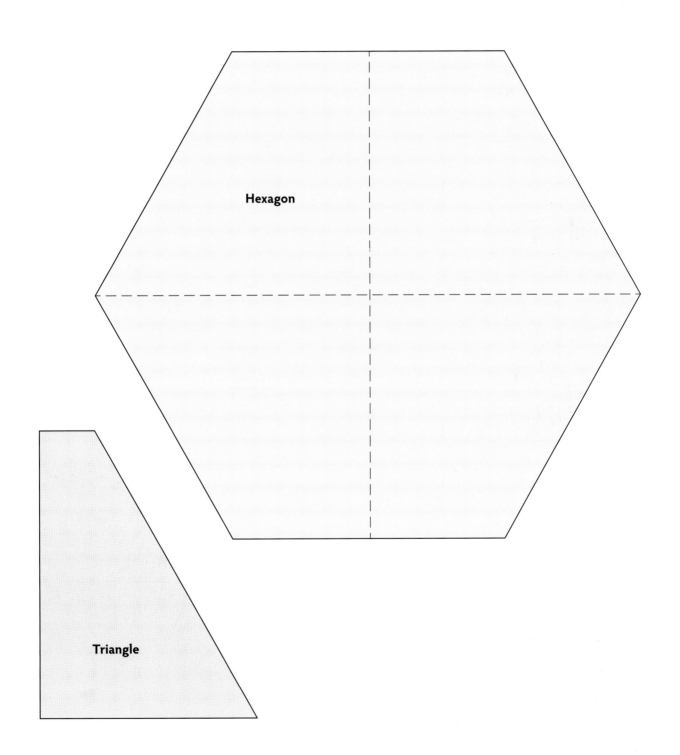

Hexagon

Triangle

"Shimmer"
Finished quilt: 60½" x 60½"
Finished block: 15" x 15"

Shimmer

I've probably made more quilts using Star blocks than any other type of block. Stars are so versatile that they can be used with just about any color combination or style of fabric. To switch things up, I added a couple extra pieces to a traditional block.

Materials

Yardage is based on 42"-wide fabric.

2⅞ yards of cream batik for blocks

1 Tonga Treats 6-Pack OR 20 strips, 6" x 42", of assorted batiks for blocks

⅝ yard of fabric for binding

4 yards of fabric for backing

68" x 68" piece of batting

Cutting

From *each* assorted batik strip, cut:*

2 squares, 6" x 6"; crosscut into 32 squares, 1½" x 1½" (640 total)

2 rectangles, 3½" x 6"; crosscut into:
4 rectangles, 1½" x 3½" (80 total; you'll have 16 extra rectangles)
1 square, 3½" x 3½" (20 total; you'll have 4 extra)

2 rectangles, 4" x 6"; crosscut into:
2 squares, 4" x 4" (40 total; you'll have 8 extra)
4 squares, 2" x 2" (80 total; you'll have 16 extra)

1 rectangle, 6" x 8"; crosscut into:
2 squares, 4" x 4" (40 total; you'll have 8 extra)
2 rectangles, 2" x 3" (40 total; you'll have 8 extra)

1 rectangle, 2" x 6"; crosscut into 2 rectangles, 2" x 3" (40 total; you'll have 8 extra)

From the cream batik, cut:

3 strips, 4½" x 42"; crosscut into 32 rectangles, 3½" x 4½"

7 strips, 4" x 42"; crosscut into 64 squares, 4" x 4"

5 strips, 3½" x 42"; crosscut into 128 rectangles, 1½" x 3½"

20 strips, 1½" x 42"; crosscut into 512 squares, 1½" x 1½"

From the fabric for binding, cut:

7 strips, 2¼" x 42"

The primary cuts will be made across the width of the strips.

Making the Blocks

1. Randomly select five batik and four cream 1½" squares. Lay out the pieces in a nine-patch setting as shown. Sew the squares together in rows. Press the seam allowances toward the batik squares. Sew the rows together and press the seam allowances away from the center of the block. Make 64 nine-patch units.

Make 64.

2. Randomly sew cream 1½" squares to opposite sides of a batik 1½" square. Press the seam allowances in one direction. Make 128 units.

Make 128.

3. Join two units from step 2 and one batik 1½" x 3½" rectangle as shown, making sure the seam allowances on the top unit are going in one direction and the seam allowances on the bottom unit are going in the opposite direction. Press the seam allowances toward the center. Make 64 Plus units.

Plus units.
Make 64.

4. Randomly select and sew together three batik 1½" squares and press the seam allowances in one direction. Sew cream 1½" x 3½" rectangles to both long edges of the pieced strip. Press the seam allowances in one direction. Make 64 Cross units.

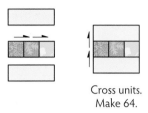

Cross units.
Make 64.

5. Mark a diagonal line from corner to corner on the wrong side of each cream 4" square. Pair each marked square right sides together with a batik 4" square. Sew ¼" from each side of the drawn line. Cut the squares apart on the drawn line, and press the seam allowances open. Make 128 half-square-triangle units. Square up each unit to measure 3½" x 3½".

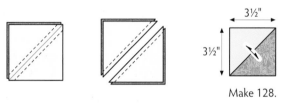

Make 128.

6. Randomly select a batik 2" square and a batik 2" x 3" rectangle. Sew the pieces together to make a pieced strip. Press the seam allowances toward the rectangle. Make 64. Sew the pieced strips together in pairs to make 32 units. Carefully clip the center of the seam allowances on each unit; clip up to, *but not through,* the stitching. Press the seam allowances away from the squares.

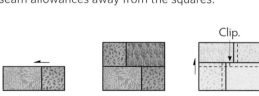

Make 64.   Make 32.

7. Lay a pieced unit from step 6 right side down on the cutting mat and align the 45° mark on the ruler with the long edge of the unit. Align the edge of the ruler with a corner of the unit and the intersection of the stitching on the corner square. Lightly draw a diagonal line. Rotate the unit 180° and mark the opposite corner. The drawn lines should be slightly more than ½" apart. Repeat to mark all of the units from step 6.

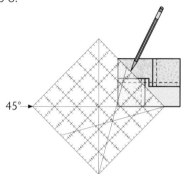

8. Place each marked unit right sides together with a cream 3½" x 4" rectangle. Stitch along each drawn line. Cut between the two stitched lines to make two corner units. Press the seam allowances toward the cream triangle. Make 64 corner units.

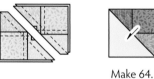

Make 64.

9. Randomly select four nine-patch units and four Plus units. Lay out the units and one batik 3½" square in three rows as shown. Join the pieces in rows. Press the seam allowances in the directions indicated. Join the rows and press the seam allowances away from the center. Make 16 center units.

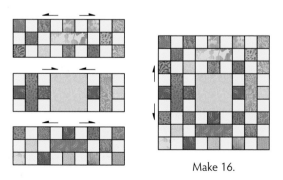

Make 16.

10. Randomly select eight half-square-triangle units, four Cross units, four corner units, and one center unit. Lay out the units as shown, paying close attention to the orientation of the half-square-triangle units. Also note that the seam allowances in the Cross units should all be going in a clockwise direction around the block. Join the units in rows as shown. Press the seam allowances in the directions indicated. Join the rows and press the seam allowances away from the center. Make a total of 16 blocks.

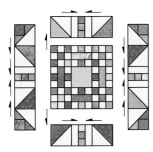 

Make 16.

Assembling the Quilt Top

1. Lay out the blocks in four rows of four blocks each as shown in the quilt assembly diagram below. Rotate and rearrange the blocks until you are satisfied with the placement. Sew the blocks together in rows. Press the seam allowances in opposite directions from row to row.

2. Sew the rows together and press the seam allowances in one direction.

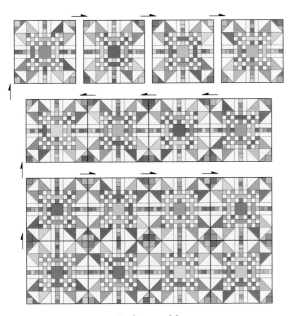

Quilt assembly

Finishing the Quilt

For more information on layering, quilting, or binding, go to ShopMartingale.com/HowtoQuilt and download free illustrated information.

1. Cut and piece the backing fabric so it measures 6" to 8" larger than the quilt top in both directions.

2. Quilt as desired. A bold quilt like this is not a good candidate for custom quilting. Instead, opt for a simple allover design with curves to soften the appearance. This quilt was quilted with a swirl design.

3. Use the 2¼"-wide binding strips to bind the quilt.

"Bitsy"
Finished quilt: 24½" x 24½"
Finished block: 3" x 3"

Bitsy

There's just something about small quilts with a big impact that is so appealing. This quilt is small. It's charming. But don't let its petite size intimidate you. The finished pieces may be small, but I have a few tricks up my sleeve to help you make it as simply and quickly as possible—starting with 5" charm squares.

Materials

Yardage is based on 42"-wide fabric.

¾ yard of tan solid for blocks and binding

40 charm squares, 5" x 5", of assorted prints for blocks

1 yard of fabric for backing

32" x 32" piece of batting

Cutting

From the tan solid, cut:

3 strips, 4¼" x 42"; crosscut into 32 rectangles, 3½" x 4¼"

3 strips, 2¼" x 42"

Making the Blocks

1. Randomly pair two print 5" squares right sides together. Sew the squares together along opposite sides to make 20 units.

Make 20.

2. Cut each unit from step 1 in half between the stitched lines to make two units measuring 2½" x 5". *Don't press.* Sew ¼" from the newly cut edge on each unit to make 40 units.

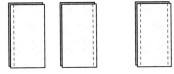

Make 40.

3. Cut each unit from step 2 in half between the stitched lines to make 80 units, each measuring 1¼" x 5". Press the seam allowances open. Randomly sew the units together in pairs, matching the long sides, to make 40 units. Press the seam allowances open. Each unit should measure 3½" x 5".

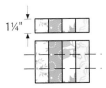

Make 40.

4. Randomly select eight units from step 3 and cut *each* of them into four segments measuring 1¼" x 3½".

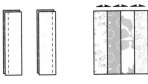

1¼"

SCRAPPY TIP

Fabric Stepchildren

It happens to us all. There is that one fabric or color in a collection that we don't really love but if we take it out, the whole color palette goes flat. So just how do you handle these difficult fabrics? I find that if I use that fabric in the smallest pieces needed for the quilt, the impact it had in a larger form disperses. Think of it as putting sprinkles on a cake rather than covering it with frosting. Sometimes things are much better in smaller packages.

5. Randomly select two of the units from step 3 and place them right sides together with the seams aligned. Sew along both 3½" edges as shown. Make 16 units. Cut each unit in half between the stitched lines. *Don't press.* Sew ¼" from the newly cut edge on each unit to make 32 units. Cut each of these in half between the stitched lines to make 64 smaller units. Press the seam allowances open.

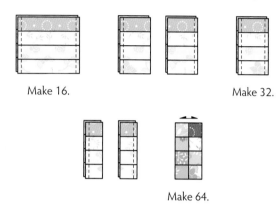

Make 16.   Make 32.

Make 64.

6. Randomly select two units from step 5 and one unit from step 4. Lay out the units so the fabrics are mixed up, rearranging as needed. Sew the units together to make a rectangular unit as shown. Press the seam allowances open. Make 32 units.

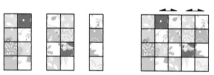

Make 32.

7. Using a pencil or a removable marker, mark a diagonal line on the wrong side of each rectangular unit, starting in the upper-right corner and running through the seam intersections to the bottom edge. In the same way, mark a line from the lower-left corner to the top edge as shown. The drawn lines should be slightly more than ½" apart. Place a marked unit right sides together with a tan 3½" x 4¼" rectangle. Stitch directly on the drawn lines, making sure to stitch through each seam intersection on the pieced unit. Cut the units apart between the stitched lines to make two blocks; trim the seam allowances to ¼" as needed. Press the seam allowances toward the tan triangle. Make 64 blocks.

Make 64.

Assembling the Quilt Top

1. Lay out the blocks in eight rows of eight blocks each, rotating every other block to create a scrappy chevron effect as shown in the quilt assembly diagram below.

2. Rearrange the blocks until you are satisfied with the mix of colors and fabrics. Sew the blocks together in rows. Press the seam allowances in opposite directions from row to row. Sew the rows together. Press the seam allowances in one direction.

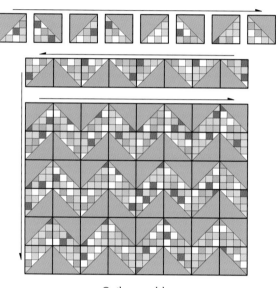

Quilt assembly

Finishing the Quilt

For more information on layering, quilting, or binding, go to ShopMartingale.com/HowtoQuilt and download free illustrated information.

1. Cut the backing fabric so it measures 6" to 8" larger than the quilt top in both directions.

2. Quilt as desired. This is a great design to play up the chevron effect. I quilted straight lines in the pieced areas and small feathers running in opposing directions in the solid chevrons.

3. Use the 2¼"-wide binding strips to bind the quilt.

Baskets

Get back to tradition with a Basket quilt featuring a Burgoyne Surrounded block. This two-color quilt (two colors, but 28 different fabrics!) shouts heritage and tradition. If it's a little too traditional for your taste, consider mixing up the color scheme with lots of bold color choices.

Materials

Yardage is based on 42"-wide fabric.

16 fat quarters (18" x 21") of assorted cream prints for blocks

12 fat eighths (9" x 21") of assorted red prints for blocks

⅝ yard of fabric for binding

4 yards of fabric for backing

65" x 65" piece of batting

SCRAPPY TIP

Tonal Variety

When making a scrappy quilt with a limited palette like this one, make sure to include plenty of variety in your fabric choices. You don't want the colors to be exactly the same value with just a variance in patterns. Look at the reds in the quilt on page 26—they vary from bright to dark, but they all work well together. Also add fabrics with similar hues. For instance, I used some reds that have rusty or coral undertones; those fabrics still read as red and blend with the chosen mix of fabrics. It's important to have fabrics that work well together, yet look independent in the mix.

Cutting

From *each* of the red prints, cut:

1 strip, 4" x 21"; crosscut into:
  1 square, 4" x 4" (12 total; you'll have 4 extra)
  5 squares, 2½" x 2½" (60 total; you'll have 8 extra)
  2 squares, 2" x 2" (24 total; you'll have 8 extra)
3 strips, 1½" x 21"; crosscut into:
  3 rectangles, 1½" x 5½" (36 total; you'll have 4 extra)
  2 rectangles, 1½" x 4½" (24 total; you'll have 8 extra)
  14 squares, 1½" x 1½" (168 total; you'll have 11 extra)

From *each* of the cream prints, cut:

1 strip, 4½" x 21"; crosscut into:
  1 square, 4¼" x 4¼" (16 total; you'll have 8 extra)
  4 rectangles, 3½" x 4½" (64 total; you'll have 8 extra)
1 strip, 4" x 21"; crosscut into:
  1 square, 4" x 4" (16 total; you'll have 8 extra)
  1 square, 2½" x 2½" (16 total)
  1 square, 2" x 2" (16 total)
  7 squares, 1½" x 1½" (112 total; you'll have 12 extra)
2 strips, 3½" x 21"; crosscut into:
  1 rectangle, 3½" x 4½" (16 total)
  11 rectangles, 2½" x 3½" (176 total)
  2 rectangles, 2" x 3½" (32 total)
1 strip, 1½" x 21"; crosscut into:
  2 rectangles, 1½" x 5½" (32 total)
  1 rectangle, 1½" x 4½" (16 total)
  2 squares, 1½" x 1½" (32 total)

From the fabric for binding, cut:

7 strips, 2¼" x 42"

"Baskets," pieced by Beth Safick and quilted by Rebecca Silbaugh
Finished quilt: 57½" x 57½"
Finished block: 24" x 24"

Making the Center Blocks

1. Mark a diagonal line from corner to corner on the wrong side of 32 red 2½" squares. With right sides together, place two marked squares on opposite corners of a cream 4¼" square, raw edges aligned. The points of the red squares will be slightly overlapped and the drawn line should extend across the large square from corner to corner as shown. Stitch ¼" from both sides of the drawn line. Cut the squares apart on the drawn line. Press the seam allowances toward the red triangles.

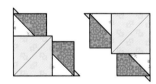

2. With right sides together, place marked red squares on the corner of each unit from step 1. The drawn line should extend from the point of the corner to the point between the two red triangles. Stitch ¼" from both sides of the drawn line. Cut the squares apart on the drawn line. Press the seam allowances toward the red triangles to make four flying-geese units. Square up each unit to measure 2" x 3½". Make a total of 32 units.

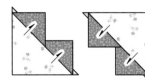

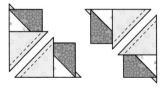

Make 32.

3. Mark a diagonal line from corner to corner on the wrong side of 16 red 2½" squares. Pair each marked square right sides together with a cream 2½" square. Stitch ¼" from both sides of the drawn line. Cut the squares apart on the drawn line to make two half-square-triangle units. Press the seam allowances toward the red triangles. Trim each unit to measure 2" x 2". Make 32 small units.

Make 32.

4. Repeat step 3, using eight red 4" squares and eight cream 4" squares to make 16 large half-square-triangle units. Press the seam allowances toward the red triangles. Trim each unit to measure 3½" x 3½".

5. Lay out two flying-geese units, two small half-square-triangle units, one large half-square-triangle unit, two cream 2" x 3½" rectangles, one red 2" square, and one cream 2" square. Sew the pieces together in sections, and then join the sections to make a Basket block as shown. Press the seam allowances in the directions indicated. The block should measure 6½" x 6½". Make 16 blocks.

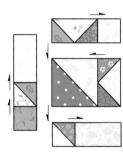 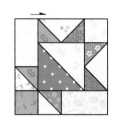

Make 16.

6. Randomly select two cream 2½" x 3½" rectangles and sew them together to make a pieced strip measuring 2½" x 6½". Press the seam allowances in one direction. Make four pieced strips. Join the pieced strips, four Basket blocks from step 5, and

one red 2½" square in rows as shown below. Press the seam allowances in the directions indicated. Sew the rows together to make a center block. Press the seam allowances toward the center. Make four.

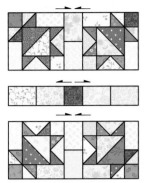

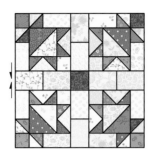

Make 4.

Assembling the Blocks

1. Sew seven cream 2½" x 3½" rectangles together side by side to make a 3½" x 14½" strip. Press the seam allowances away from the center of the unit as shown. Make 16 pieced strips.

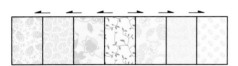

Make 16.

2. Sew two red and two cream 1½" squares together to make a four-patch unit. Press the seam allowances in the directions indicated. Make 16 units.

Make 16.

3. Sew five red and four cream 1½" squares together to make a nine-patch unit. Press the seam allowances in the directions indicated. Make 25 units.

Make 25.

4. Sew together one four-patch unit, one nine-patch unit, and two cream 2½" x 3½" rectangles to make a corner unit. Make 16 units.

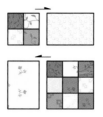 

Make 16.

5. Sew together a red 1½" x 5½" rectangle and a cream 1½" x 5½" rectangle along their long edges. Press the seam allowances toward the red rectangle. Make 32 units.

Make 32.

6. Sew together a red 1½" x 4½" rectangle and a cream 1½" x 4½" rectangle along their long edges. Press the seam allowances toward the red rectangle. Make 16. Sew two 5½"-long units from step 5 and one 4½"-long unit together, alternating the colors as shown. Press the seam allowances toward the center. Make 16 units.

Make 16.

7. Lay out four pieced strips from step 1, four corner units from step 4, four units from step 6, and one center block as shown. Sew the pieces together in rows, and then sew the rows together. Press the seam allowances in the directions indicated. Make four blocks.

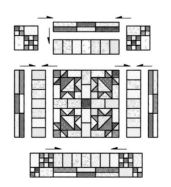 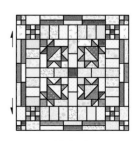

Make 4.

Assembling the Quilt Top

1. Join six cream 3½" x 4½" rectangles end to end to make a 3½" x 24½" sashing strip. Press the seam allowances in one direction. Make 12 sashing strips.

2. Lay out the blocks, sashing strips, and nine remaining nine-patch units as shown in the quilt assembly diagram below. Sew the pieces together in rows. Press the seam allowances toward the sashing strips. Sew the rows together. Press the seam allowances toward the sashing strips.

Finishing the Quilt

For more information on layering, quilting, or binding, go to ShopMartingale.com/HowtoQuilt and download free illustrated information.

1. Cut and piece the backing fabric so it measures 6" to 8" larger than the quilt top in both directions.

2. Quilt as desired. Some quilts with large areas of background to "play in," like this one, are optimal for custom quilting. With this quilt's traditional flair, it would be a great canvas for feathers and other traditional elements. I quilted a mixture of modern straight lines and traditional feathers.

3. Use the 2¼"-wide binding strips to bind the quilt.

Quilt assembly

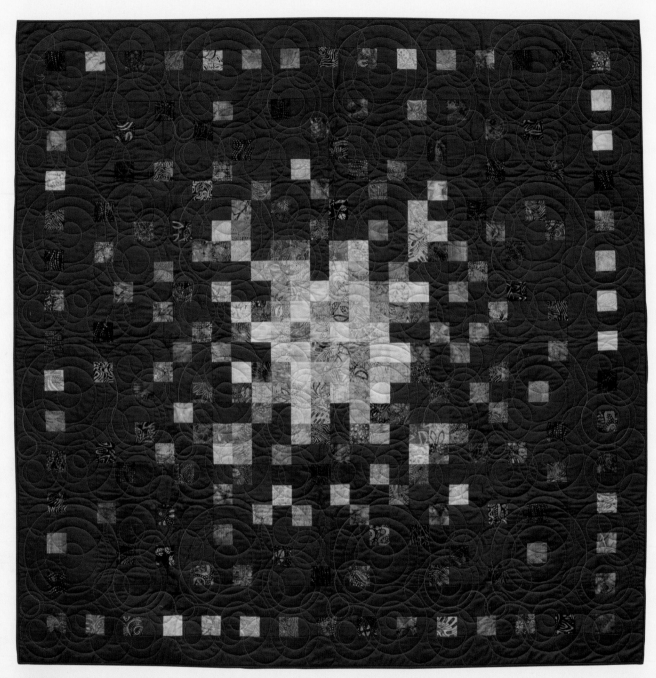

"Nova," pieced by Rebecca Silbaugh and quilted by Abby Latimer of Latimer Lane Quilting
Finished quilt: 64½" x 64½"
Finished block: 6" x 6"

Nova

As long as I've been quilting, I've wanted to make a pixel-style quilt. Finally, here it is! It looks complex, but it's really quite simple. I blended a solid with batiks and let the color do the talking, but this pattern would also look great made using bright prints for a child's quilt or neutrals for a more masculine quilt.

Materials

Yardage is based on 42"-wide fabric.

3½ yards of gray solid for blocks and borders

65 charm squares, 5" x 5", of assorted batiks for blocks and pieced border

⅝ yard of fabric for binding

4 yards of fabric for backing

72" x 72" piece of batting

Cutting

From *each* assorted batik square, cut:

    4 squares, 2½" x 2½" (260 total)

From the gray solid, cut:

    3 strips, 6½" x 42"; crosscut into 36 rectangles, 2½" x 6½"

    7 strips, 4½" x 42"; crosscut into 112 rectangles, 2½" x 4½"

    12 strips, 3½" x 42"

    6 strips, 2½" x 42"; crosscut into 96 squares, 2½" x 2½"

From the fabric for binding, cut:

    7 strips, 2¼" x 42"

Making the Blocks

To create the same glowing look as I did, sort the charm squares into piles of lights, mediums, and darks. I started creating my blocks with the lighter squares and moved to the darker ones. I also pulled out random squares for the border ahead of time, so the squares had a nice mix of values as well.

1. Randomly select nine batik 2½" squares and stitch them together in a nine-patch setting. Make four A blocks.

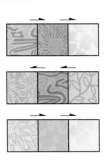
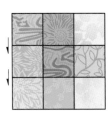

Block A.
Make 4.

2. Randomly select five batik 2½" squares and two gray 2½" x 4½" rectangles. Sew four squares together to make a four-patch unit. Sew the four-patch unit, gray rectangles, and remaining square in rows, and then join the rows. Press the seam allowances in the directions indicated. Make 12 B blocks.

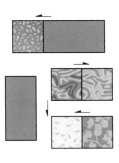
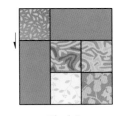

Block B.
Make 12.

3. Sew a batik 2½" square to the end of a gray 2½" x 4½" rectangle. Press the seam allowances toward the square. Make 88 units.

Make 88.

4. Sew gray 2½" squares to opposite sides of a batik 2½" square. Press the seam allowances toward the batik square. Make 20 units.

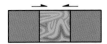

Make 20.

5. Randomly select two units from step 3 and one unit from step 4. Sew the units together to make a 6½" x 6½" block. Press the seam allowances in one direction. Make 16 C blocks.

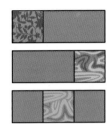 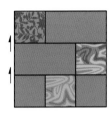

Block C.
Make 16.

6. Randomly select two units from step 3. Sew the units and one gray 2½" x 6½" rectangle together to make a block. Press the seam allowances in one direction. Make 20 D blocks. Repeat the process to make eight E blocks, making sure to orient the units as shown.

 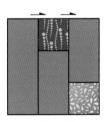

Block D.
Make 20.

Block E.
Make 8.

7. Sew gray 2½" x 6½" rectangles to both long edges of each remaining unit from step 4 to make four F blocks. Press the seam allowances in one direction.

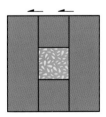

Block F.
Make 4.

Crayon-Box Theory

When you see a fabric on its own, it can be so powerful that it's overwhelming. (You may even think it's hideous.) But in the right context, this fabric can be tamed and beautiful. Why does this happen? I liken it to a crayon box.

Think about some of the crazy colors crayons come in. Whether they're too bright, too dull, or too "whatever" for your taste, they are there for a reason. When those crayons are in the box, their colors add to the beauty of the grouping.

In this quilt, that peachy color was giving me fits, but if I took it out, the whole quilt looked flat. Now that the quilt is complete, I can't picture it without this color. So before you toss out a color from your precut bundle, think about a box of crayons.

Assembling the Quilt Top

There are two ways to tackle this quilt. I designed this quilt in quadrants. Each quadrant is constructed the same way, and is simply rotated 90° or 180° to form the design. If you prefer, you can lay out the blocks in eight rows and then sew the blocks together in rows to assemble the quilt. Sewing quadrants is less daunting for some people than working with long rows, but laying out the blocks into rows first allows for more control over the color placement.

1. For each quadrant, lay out one A block, three B blocks, four C blocks, five D blocks, two E blocks, and one F block in four rows, making sure to orient the blocks as shown on page 33. Rearrange the blocks until you're satisfied with the color placement.

2. Sew the blocks together in rows. Press the seam allowances in opposite directions from row to row. Join the rows and press the seam allowances in one direction. Make four quadrants.

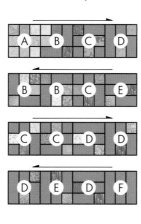

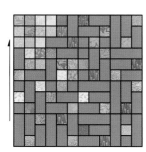

Make 4.

3. Lay out the four quadrants, rotating them as shown in the quilt assembly diagram at right. Sew the quadrants together in rows. Press the seam allowances in opposite directions from row to row. Join the rows and press the seam allowances in one direction.

4. Sew gray 3½"-wide strips end to end to make a long strip. Measure the length of the quilt top through the middle and near both edges; determine the average of these measurements. Cut two strips to the average length. Sew these strips to the sides of the quilt, matching the ends and easing in any excess. Press the seam allowances toward the border strips.

5. Measure the width of the quilt top through the middle and near both edges; determine the average of these measurements. From the pieced gray strip, cut two strips to the average width. Sew these strips to the top and bottom of the quilt, matching the ends and easing in any excess. Press the seam allowances toward the border strips.

6. For the pieced border, sew 14 gray and 13 batik 2½" squares together, beginning and ending with a gray square, to make a side border. Press the seam allowances in one direction. Make two side borders. For the top border, sew 15 batik and 14 gray 2½" squares together, beginning and ending with a batik square. Press the seam allowances in one direction. Repeat to make a bottom border. Sew the borders to the sides first, and then the top, and bottom of the quilt top as shown in the quilt assembly diagram.

7. Repeat steps 4 and 5 to add the remaining gray 3½"-wide strips to the quilt top for the outer border.

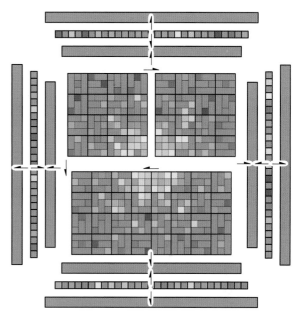

Quilt assembly

Finishing the Quilt

For more information on layering, quilting, or binding, go to ShopMartingale.com/HowtoQuilt and download free illustrated information.

1. Cut and piece the backing fabric so it measures 6" to 8" larger than the quilt top in both directions.

2. Quilt as desired. I had an amazing design in my head of how to finish this quilt with tons of quilted circles, but I couldn't figure out how to do it until I saw an incredible computerized design. It was perfect and the quilted circles soften the geometric appearance of the quilt.

3. Use the 2¼"-wide binding strips to bind the quilt.

"Tic Tac Tile," pieced by Rebecca Silbaugh and quilted by Steve Kooistra
Finished quilt: 64½" x 80½"
Finished block: 8" x 8"

Tic Tac Tile

Honestly, this quilt turned out completely different than the image I had in my mind when I started, but that's okay! Depending on the fabrics you use, your version can take on a whole new look simply by choosing a bolder color for the sashing than I did. Simple and versatile, here's a pattern that's suited to any number of fabric combinations.

Materials

Yardage is based on 42"-wide fabric unless otherwise noted.

1 Jelly Roll OR 40 strips, 2½" x 42", of brown solid for blocks

1 Layer Cake OR 40 squares, 10" x 10", of assorted light or medium prints for blocks

⅔ yard of fabric for binding

5 yards of fabric for backing

72" x 88" piece of batting

Cutting

From *each* brown-solid strip, cut:
    2 rectangles, 2½" x 8½" (80 total)
    2 rectangles, 2½" x 4½" (80 total)
    4 squares, 2½" x 2½" (160 total)

From *each* light- or medium-print square, cut:
    1 strip, 4½" x 10"; crosscut into:
        1 square, 4½" x 4½" (40 total)
        2 rectangles, 2½" x 4½" (80 total)
    1 rectangle, 4½" x 8½" (40 total)

From the fabric for binding, cut:
    8 strips, 2¼" x 42"

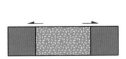

SCRAPPY TIP

Themes

To keep scrappy quilts looking cohesive rather than like a hot mess, it's best to have a theme. Using precuts makes this easy since the fabrics all came from the same line and already have a theme. But what if you're choosing your own fabrics? Consider using primarily florals, working in a limited color palette, or sticking with a particular style of fabric, such as batiks, modern prints, or Civil War reproductions. One caveat: some of the best scrappy quilts have no theme at all. They fall under the "everyone in the pool" mentality. Whatever route you follow, remember to relax and have fun!

Making the Blocks

Use one light (or medium) print for each block.

1. Sew brown 2½" squares to both ends of a light 2½" x 4½" rectangle. Press the seam allowances toward the squares. Make two units. Sew the units to both long edges of a light 4½" x 8½" rectangle. Press the seam allowances toward the center of the block. Repeat to make 40 A blocks.

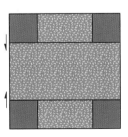

Block A.
Make 40.

2. Sew brown 2½" x 4½" rectangles to opposite sides of a light 4½" square. Press the seam allowances toward the dark rectangles. Sew brown 2½" x 8½" rectangles to the top and the bottom of each unit. Press the seam allowances toward the dark rectangles. Repeat to make 40 B blocks.

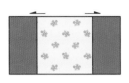
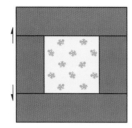

Block B.
Make 40.

Assembling the Quilt Top

1. Randomly select one A block and one B block and sew them together as shown to make a half block. Press the seam allowances toward the B block. Make 40.

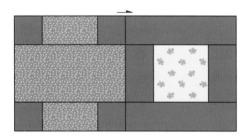

Make 40.

2. Sew two half-blocks together to make one large block. Carefully clip the seam allowances at the intersection of the blocks; clip up to, *but not through,* the stitching. Press the seam allowances in a clockwise direction. Make 20 blocks.

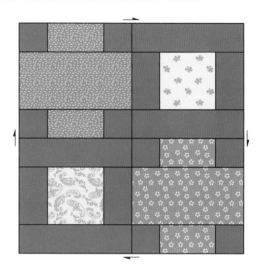

Make 20.

3. Lay out the blocks in five rows of four blocks each, making sure to orient the blocks as shown in the quilt assembly diagram below. Rearrange the blocks until you're pleased with the arrangement. Sew the blocks together in rows. Press the seam allowances in opposite directions from row to row. Sew the rows together. Press the seam allowances in one direction.

Finishing the Quilt

For more information on layering, quilting, or binding, go to ShopMartingale.com/HowtoQuilt and download free illustrated information.

1. Cut and piece the backing fabric so it measures 6" to 8" larger than the quilt top in both directions.

2. Quilt as desired. Depending on the fabrics you use, this quilt could be quilted with either an awesome custom design or a good allover texture design. I quilted a combination of pebbles and swirls to give the quilt texture but not another design element.

3. Use the 2¼"-wide binding strips to bind the quilt.

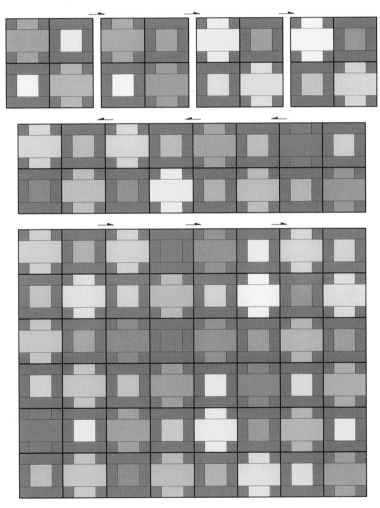

Qulit assembly

"Frolic"
Finished quilt: 72½" x 72½"
Finished block: 12" x 12"

Frolic

In my quest to get back to the basics of quilting, I have a bucket list of quilts I'd like to make. (C'mon, I bet you do, too.) A Log Cabin quilt was high on my list. I like the idea of making the center of the block more than just a plain square, and you'll notice that my Log Cabin's style is more reminiscent of reclaimed wood than modular housing, as my "logs" aren't always even.

Materials

Yardage is based on 42"-wide fabric.

18 fat quarters (18" x 21") of assorted light prints for blocks

18 fat quarters of bold prints for blocks

⅝ yard of fabric for binding

4½ yards of fabric for backing

80" x 80" piece of batting

Cutting

From *each* of the assorted light prints, cut:

    5 strips, 2" x 21"; crosscut into:
        2 rectangles, 2" x 11½" (36 total)
        2 rectangles, 2" x 10" (36 total)
        2 rectangles, 2" x 6½" (36 total)
        2 rectangles, 2" x 5" (36 total)
        4 rectangles, 2" x 2½" (72 total)
        4 rectangles, 1½" x 2" (72 total)
    2 strips, 1½" x 21"; crosscut into:
        2 rectangles, 1½" x 8½" (36 total)
        2 rectangles, 1½" x 7½" (36 total)

From *each* of the bold prints, cut:

    1 strip, 2½" x 21"; crosscut into:
        2 squares, 2½" x 2½" (36 total)
        4 rectangles, 1½" x 2½" (72 total)
        2 squares, 2" x 2" (36 total)
        2 squares, 1½" x 1½" (36 total)
    2 strips, 2" x 21"; crosscut into:
        2 rectangles, 2" x 10" (36 total)
        2 rectangles, 2" x 8½" (36 total)
    4 strips, 1½" x 21"; crosscut into:
        2 rectangles, 1½" x 12½" (36 total)
        2 rectangles, 1½" x 11½" (36 total)
        2 rectangles, 1½" x 7½" (36 total)
        2 rectangles, 1½" x 6½" (36 total)

From the fabric for binding, cut:

    8 strips, 2¼" x 42"

Making the Blocks

1. For each wonky Nine Patch block, you'll need the following pieces from one bold print: one 1½" square, one 2" square, one 2½" square, and two 1½" x 2½" rectangles. From the light prints, randomly select two 1½" x 2" rectangles and two 2" x 2½" rectangles. Lay out the pieces in three rows as shown. Sew the pieces together in rows. Press the seam allowances toward the bold fabrics. Sew the rows together and press the seam allowances away from the center. The block should measure 5" x 5". Make 36 blocks.

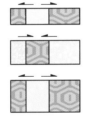

Make 36.

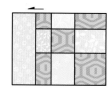

Salad Bowl/Sprinkler Toss

When making a scrappy quilt, you may need to switch from organized cut piles to randomly assorted pieces. I find that gently mixing the fabrics helps keep things random, and it's a great activity to do while watching TV and prepping for a day of quilting. Start by tossing the pieces onto the floor or table one at a time, moving slightly back and forth as you toss, like a sprinkler. Then, if the pieces need a little extra mixing, use your hands to scoop and flip the pieces like tossing a salad. The key is to be gentle. Gather the pieces by grabbing either the piece closest to you or the piece on top of the pile. You can also do this with units or finished blocks if needed. It's quite relaxing and gives great results. Give it a try!

2. To make sewing the blocks together more efficient, stack the remaining rectangles in the order they will be used, with the largest rectangle on bottom and the smallest rectangle on the top. Stack the rectangles in the following order:

   Bold: 1½" x 12½"

   Bold: 1½" x 11½"

   Light: 2" x 11½"

   Light: 2" x 10"

   Bold: 2" x 10"

   Bold: 2" x 8½"

   Light: 1½" x 8½"

   Light: 1½" x 7½"

   Bold: 1½" x 7½"

   Bold: 1½" x 6½"

   Light: 2" x 6½"

   Light: 2" x 5"

3. Randomly select a light 2" x 5" rectangle and sew it to the left side of a wonky Nine Patch block. Press the seam allowances toward the rectangle.

4. Randomly select a light 2" x 6½" rectangle and sew it to the top of the block. Press the seam allowances toward the rectangle.

5. Continue in the same way, adding rectangles around the center block in a clockwise direction. The light prints should always be added to the top and left of the center block, and the bold print should always be added to the right and bottom. Press the seam allowances toward each newly added rectangle. Make 36 blocks.

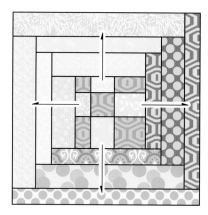

Make 36.

Assembling the Quilt Top

1. Lay out the blocks in six rows of six blocks each, rotating the blocks to achieve the desired look and making sure the colors are balanced and well mixed. Refer to the photo on page 38 and the quilt assembly diagram on page 41 for placement guidance. Sew the blocks together in rows. Press the seam allowances in opposite directions from row to row.

2. Join the rows and press the seam allowances in one direction.

Viewpoint

If you're unsure of your fabric pairings or the layout of your quilt, look at the project over your shoulder using a mirror. It sounds goofy but it tricks your brain, allowing you to see colors more clearly or areas of trouble you couldn't see looking at the quilt straight on. We get used to seeing things a certain way and this is a fast and easy way to get a new perspective. Another option is to take a picture with a phone or digital camera. Often the digital image distorts colors and acts like a filter to your brain. Give these techniques a try the next time you feel stuck.

Finishing the Quilt

For more information on layering, quilting, or binding, go to ShopMartingale.com/HowtoQuilt and download free illustrated information.

1. Cut and piece the backing fabric so it measures 6" to 8" larger than the quilt top in both directions.

2. Quilt as desired. To highlight the rows and dimension of this quilt, I alternated quilting motifs in the light and bold areas. Lighter areas show off more detail, so feathers grace those areas, while a geometric design gives texture to the bold prints.

3. Use the 2¼"-wide binding strips to bind the quilt.

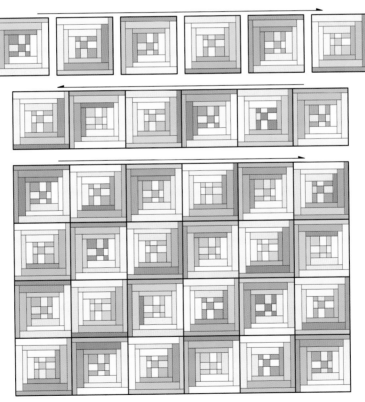

Quilt assembly

"Medley," pieced by Rebecca Silbaugh and quilted by Steve Kooistra
Finished quilt: 62½" x 86½"
Finished block: 6" x 6"

Medley

Every once in awhile I get a crazy idea to play with new fabric combinations. The best way I've found to do that successfully has been to start with a simple pattern. For example, by focusing simply on Nine Patch blocks, I can play as much as I want with the colors and fabrics, and if I get out of line, a good border can always tie the quilt together.

Materials

Yardage is based on 42"-wide fabric.

24 fat eighths (9" x 21") of assorted prints for blocks and pieced border

1⅝ yards of orange print for outer border

1½ yards of black print for sashing and inner border

1¼ yards of light print for sashing

⅝ yard of fabric for binding

5⅓ yards of fabric for backing

70" x 94" piece of batting

Cutting

From *each* of the assorted prints, cut:

2 squares, 7½" x 7½" (48 total)

2 squares, 2½" x 2½" (48 total; you'll have 2 extra squares)

From the black print, cut:

12 strips, 2½" x 42"; crosscut *3 of the strips* into 35 squares, 2½" x 2½"

11 strips, 1½" x 42"; crosscut into 280 squares, 1½" x 1½"

From the light print, cut:

6 strips, 6½" x 42"; crosscut into 82 rectangles, 2½" x 6½"

From the orange print, cut:

8 strips, 6½" x 42"

From the fabric for binding, cut:

8 strips, 2¼" x 42"

Making the Blocks

For this quilt, you'll make five different styles of Nine Patch blocks.

1. To make the first block, randomly select 10 print 7½" squares. Stack two or three squares (whatever you feel comfortable cutting through) on a cutting mat. Use a rotary cutter to cut the squares twice vertically and horizontally to make nine 2½" squares. Continue in the same way until you have nine stacks of 10 squares each. The squares in each stack should be in the same order.

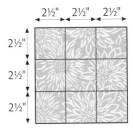

2. Move the top square on alternating stacks to the bottom of the stack. Then, using the top square in each stack, sew the squares together in rows. Press the seam allowances toward the darker squares. Sew the rows together. Press the seam allowances in one direction. Make 10 A blocks.

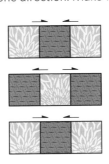
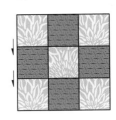

Block A.
Make 10.

Mixing Textures

Just like playing with new color combinations, from time to time I mix different fabric styles and textures in a quilt—like in this one. "Medley" is a mix of Civil War reproduction prints and various batiks. There's no rule stating that you can only use one fabric style in a quilt. The colors I chose for this quilt are so rich, and the result wouldn't be possible if I didn't mix two diverse types of fabric.

3. Randomly select 10 print 7½" squares for block B. Stack the squares in the same way as before. Measuring 2" from each edge, cut the squares twice vertically and horizontally as shown to make nine stacks. As before, move the top piece on alternating stacks to the bottom of the stack. Using the top piece in each stack, sew the pieces together in rows. Press the seam allowances toward the darker pieces. Sew the rows together. Press the seam allowances in one direction. Make 10 B blocks.

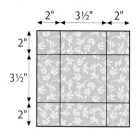
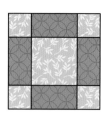

Block B.
Make 10.

4. Randomly select 10 print 7½" squares for block C. Stack the squares and, measuring 3" from each edge, cut the squares twice vertically and horizontally as shown to make nine stacks. Shift the top piece on alternating stacks to the bottom of the stack. Using the top piece in each stack, sew the pieces together in rows. Press the seam allowances toward the darker pieces. Sew the

rows together. Press the seam allowances in one direction. Make 10 C blocks.

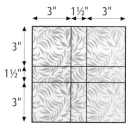

Block C.
Make 10.

5. For block D, randomly select nine print 7½" squares. Stack the squares, measure 1½" from the left edge, and make the first cut. Measuring 2½" from the first cut, make a second cut. Make one horizontal cut 1½" from the top edge and make a second cut 2½" from the first cut. Shift the top piece on alternating stacks to the bottom of the stack. Using the top piece in each stack, sew the pieces together in rows. Press the seam allowances toward the darker pieces. Sew the rows together. Press the seam allowances in one direction. Make nine D blocks.

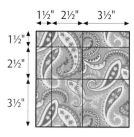
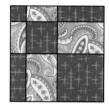

Block D.
Make 9.

6. Stack the remaining nine print 7½" squares. Measure 2" from the edge and make two vertical cuts on opposite sides as shown on page 45. Measuring 3" from the top and bottom edges, make two horizontal cuts on opposite sides. Shift the top piece on alternating stacks to the bottom of the stack. Using the top piece in each stack, sew the pieces together in rows. Press the seam allowances toward the darker squares. Sew the rows together. Press the seam allowances in one direction. Make nine E blocks.

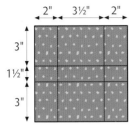
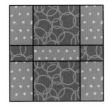

Block E.
Make 9.

Assembling the Quilt Top

1. Mark a diagonal line from corner to corner on the wrong side of each black 1½" square. Place a marked square on one corner of a light 2½" x 6½" rectangle, right sides together, as shown. Sew along the drawn line and trim the excess corner fabric, leaving a ¼" seam allowance. Press the seam allowances toward the resulting black triangle. Repeat the process, sewing a marked square on the adjacent corner of the rectangle as shown. Make 24 outer-sashing units.

Make 24.

2. Using the remaining marked squares from step 1, sew black squares to each corner of a light 2½" x 6½" rectangle as shown. Make 58 interior sashing units.

Make 58.

3. Randomly lay out the blocks, sashing units, and black 2½" squares as shown in the quilt assembly diagram on page 46. Rotate some of the blocks to give the quilt dimension since many of the blocks seem to have a direction or weighted side. When you are pleased with the arrangement, sew the pieces together in rows. Press the seam allowances toward the blocks and black squares. Sew the rows together and press the seam allowances toward the block rows.

4. Join the remaining black 2½"-wide strips end to end to make a long strip. Measure the width of the quilt top through the middle and near both edges; determine the average of these measurements. From the pieced strip, cut two strips to the average width. Sew these strips to the top and bottom of the quilt, matching the ends and easing in any excess. Press the seam allowances toward the border strips.

5. Sew 23 print 2½" squares together randomly to make a pieced strip. Press the seam allowances in one direction. Make two and sew the strips to the top and bottom of the quilt. Press the seam allowances toward the black strips.

6. Measure the length of the quilt top through the middle and near both edges; determine the average of these measurements. From the pieced black strip, cut two strips to the average length. Sew these strips to the sides of the quilt, matching the ends and easing in any excess. Press the seam allowances toward the border strips.

7. Repeat step 4, using the remainder of the pieced black strip to add the top and bottom borders. Repeat steps 4 and 6 to add the orange outer border to the quilt top.

Finishing the Quilt

For more information on layering, quilting, or binding, go to ShopMartingale.com/HowtoQuilt and download free illustrated information.

1. Cut and piece the backing fabric so it measures 6" to 8" larger than the quilt top in both directions.

2. Quilt as desired. On occasion, simple quilts ask for simple quilting. Once I finished this quilt, it begged to have traditional Baptist fans quilted across it, and I love how it turned out.

3. Use the 2¼"-wide binding strips to bind the quilt.

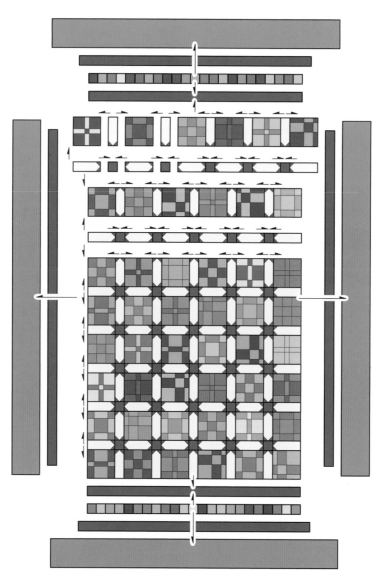

Quilt assembly

Baby Cakes

Simple can be good. Great in fact. Less truly is more. Not every quilt needs 200 fabrics and complex details. Granted, I have and love my fair share of complex quilts. (I wouldn't have created this book without those influences.) However, this quilt is an excellent example of how scrappy can also be simple.

Materials

Yardage is based on 42"-wide fabric.

1 Layer Cake *OR* 35 squares, 10" x 10" of assorted prints for blocks

½ yard of fabric for binding

2¾ yards of fabric for backing

48" x 64" piece of batting

Cutting

From *each* assorted print square, cut:
- 1 strip, 1½" x 10"; crosscut into:
  - 1 square, 1½" x 1½" (35 total)
  - 2 rectangles, 1½" x 2½" (72 total)
  - 1 rectangle, 1½" x 3½" (35 total)

From the remaining 8½" length of *each* print square, cut:
- 1 rectangle, 3" x 8½" (35 total)
- 1 rectangle, 2½" x 8½" (35 total)
- 1 rectangle, 2" x 8½" (35 total)
- 1 rectangle, 1½" x 8½" (35 total)

From the fabric for binding, cut:
- 6 strips, 2¼" x 42"

Making the Blocks

1. Randomly select one print 1½" square, two print 1½" x 2½" rectangles, and one print 1½" x 3½" rectangle. Sew the pieces together to make a 1½" x 8½" strip. It doesn't matter what order the pieces go in; just lay them out in an order where the fabrics "play well together." Press the seam allowances in one direction. Make 35 pieced strips.

Make 35.

2. Randomly select one print 1½" x 8½" rectangle, one print 2" x 8½" rectangle, one print 2½" x 8½" rectangle, and one print 3" x 8½" rectangle. Randomly sew the rectangles and a pieced strip from step 1 together to make a block. The order doesn't matter; just have fun with it. Press the seam allowances toward each newly added piece. Make 35 blocks.

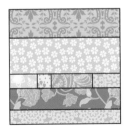

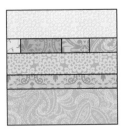

Make 35.

"Baby Cakes"
Finished quilt: 40½" x 56½"
Finished block: 8" x 8"

Assembling the Quilt Top

1. Lay out the blocks in seven rows of five blocks each as shown in the quilt assembly diagram below. Rotate alternating blocks 90° so half of the blocks run horizontally and the other half run vertically.

2. Sew the blocks together in rows. Press the seam allowances toward the vertical blocks. Sew the rows together. Press the seam allowances away from the center of the quilt.

Finishing the Quilt

For more information on layering, quilting, or binding, go to ShopMartingale.com/HowtoQuilt and download free illustrated information.

1. Cut and piece the backing fabric so it measures 6" to 8" larger than the quilt top in both directions.

2. Quilt as desired. With all of the busy prints in this quilt, it's hard to see the quilting detail, so I quilted a swirly wave pattern to add texture. It's not worth putting a bunch of work into the quilting if you can't see it.

3. Use the 2¼"-wide binding strips to bind the quilt.

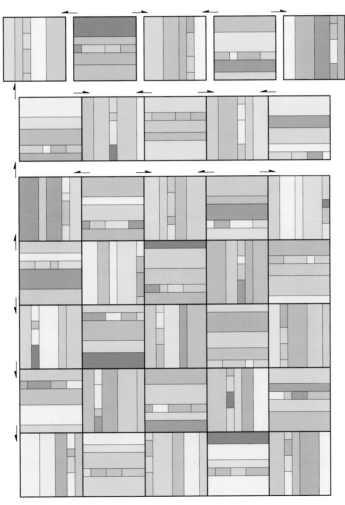

Quilt assembly

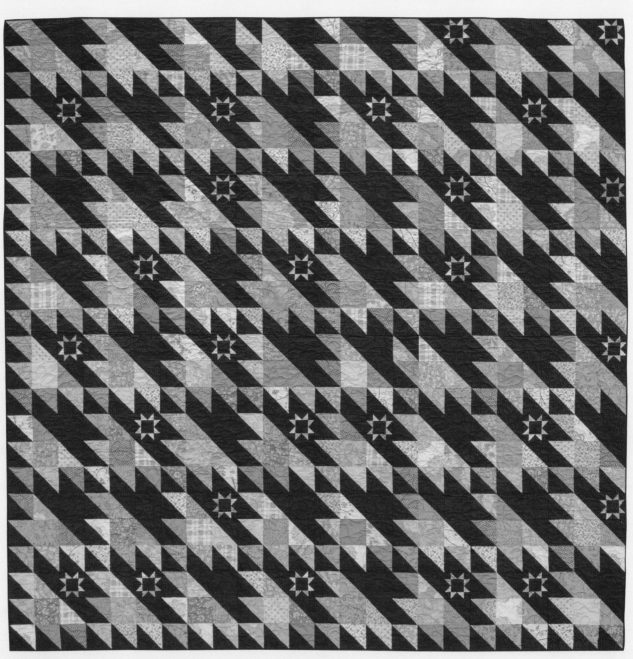

"Annabelle"
Finished quilt: 96½" x 96½"
Finished block: 12" x 12"

Annabelle

To add some charm and keep the quilt from being too simple, I added mini stars to some of the blocks and scattered them throughout the layout. This traditional quilt design is often made in just two colors; I used a mix of light-value and tone-on-tone prints for the background, rather than just one light fabric, to give the design a little more personality.

Materials

Yardage is based on 42"-wide fabric.

26 fat quarters (18" x 21") of assorted light prints for blocks

5⅔ yards of red print for blocks

⅞ yard of fabric for binding

9 yards of fabric for backing

104" x 104" piece of batting

Cutting

From *each* of 13 assorted light prints, cut:
    3 strips, 5" x 21"; crosscut into:
        10 squares, 5" x 5" (130 total; you'll have 10 extra squares)
        1 square, 4½" x 4½" (13 total)

From *each* of the remaining 13 assorted light prints, cut:
    2 strips, 5" x 21"; crosscut into 8 squares, 5" x 5" (104 total)
    1 strip, 4½" x 21"; crosscut into 4 squares, 4½" x 4½" (52 total; you'll have 1 extra)
    1 strip, 2" x 21"; crosscut into 8 squares, 2" x 2" (104 total)

From the red print, cut:
    28 strips, 5" x 42"; crosscut into 224 squares, 5" x 5"
    5 strips, 4½" x 42"; crosscut into 38 squares, 4½" x 4½"
    2 strips, 2½" x 42"; crosscut into 26 squares, 2½" x 2½"
    6 strips, 2" x 42"; crosscut into 104 squares, 2" x 2"
    4 strips, 1½" x 42"; crosscut into 104 squares, 1½" x 1½"

From the fabric for binding, cut:
    10 strips, 2¼" x 42"

Making the Blocks

1. Mark a diagonal line from corner to corner on the wrong side of each light 2" square. Pair each marked light square right sides together with a red 2" square. Sew ¼" from each side of the drawn line. Cut the squares apart on the drawn line, and press the seam allowances open. Make 208 half-square-triangle units. Square up each unit to measure 1½" x 1½".

Make 208.

2. Randomly select two half-square-triangle units from step 1 and sew them together to resemble a flying-geese unit. Press the seam allowances open. Make 104 units.

Make 104.

3. Lay out four units from step 2, four red 1½" squares, and one red 2½" square in three rows as shown. Join the pieces in rows and then join the rows to make a Star block. Press the seam allowances in the directions indicated. Make 26 blocks.

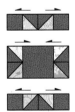

Make 26.

4. Mark a diagonal line from corner to corner on the wrong side of each light 5" square. Randomly pair each marked square right sides together with a red 5" square and stitch ¼" from each side of the drawn line. Cut the squares apart on the drawn line. Press the seam allowances open. Make 448 half-square-triangle units. Square up each unit to measure 4½" x 4½".

Make 448.

5. Lay out one Star block, seven half-square-triangle units from step 4, and one light 4½" square in three rows as shown. Sew the pieces together in rows. Press the seam allowances in opposite directions from row to row. Sew the rows together. Press the seam allowances open. Make 26 blocks.

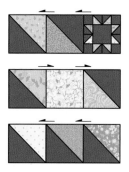
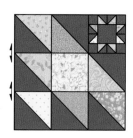

Make 26.

6. For the remaining blocks, lay out one red 4½" square, seven half-square-triangle units from step 4, and one light 4½" square in three rows as shown. Sew the pieces together in rows. Press the seam allowances in opposite directions from row to row. Sew the rows together. Press the seam allowances open. Make 38 blocks.

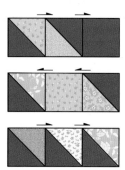
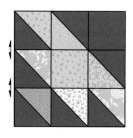

Make 38.

Assembling the Quilt Top

Lay out the blocks in eight rows of eight blocks each, randomly mixing in the star blocks. Rearrange the blocks until you're satisfied with the placement. Sew the blocks together in rows. Press the seam allowances in opposite directions from row to row. Sew the rows together. Press the seam allowances in one direction.

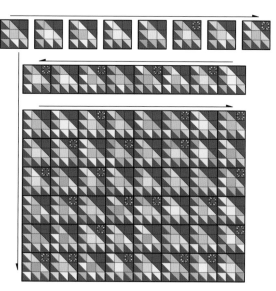

Quilt assembly

Finishing the Quilt

For more information on layering, quilting, or binding, go to ShopMartingale.com/HowtoQuilt and download free illustrated information.

1. Cut and piece the backing fabric so it measures 6" to 8" larger than the quilt top in both directions.

2. Quilt as desired. With such a bold color scheme in this quilt, I kept the quilting simple yet classic with an overall leaf design.

3. Use the 2¼"-wide binding strips to bind the quilt.

Dot Plus Dash

Some quilt blocks form a secondary pattern when they're set together. Here, adding simple sashing between the blocks lets a Shoo Fly pattern emerge at the block intersections. From a simple block, you can create an interesting—and intricate-looking—design.

Materials

Yardage is based on 42"-wide fabric.

3⅝ yards of tan linen for blocks and sashing

1 Layer Cake *OR* 40 squares, 10" x 10", of assorted prints for blocks and cornerstones

1 yard of orange print for borders

⅝ yard of fabric for binding

5 yards of fabric for backing

73" x 87" piece of batting

Cutting

From *each* of the assorted print squares, cut:
- 2 strips, 3" x 10"; crosscut into:
  - 4 squares, 3" x 3" (160 total)
  - 1 square, 2½" x 2½" (40 total)
  - 2 squares, 1½" x 1½" (80 total)
- 1 strip, 2½" x 10"; crosscut into:
  - 1 square, 2½" x 2½" (40 total)
  - 5 rectangles, 1½" x 2½" (200 total)
- 1 strip, 1½" x 10"; crosscut into:
  - 3 rectangles, 1½" x 2½" (120 total)
  - 1 square, 1½" x 1½" (40 total, you'll have 21 extra)

From the tan linen, cut:
- 7 strips, 6½" x 42"; crosscut into 178 rectangles, 1½" x 6½"
- 13 strips, 3" x 42"; crosscut into 160 squares, 3" x 3"
- 13 strips, 2½" x 42"; crosscut into 320 rectangles, 1½" x 2½"

From the orange print, cut:
- 7 strips, 4½" x 42"

From the fabric for binding, cut:
- 8 strips, 2¼" x 42"

Making the Blocks

1. Mark a diagonal line from corner to corner on the wrong side of each tan 3" square. Pair each marked square right sides together with a print 3" square. Stitch ¼" from each side of the drawn line. Cut the squares apart on the drawn line, and press the seam allowances toward the print triangle. Make 320 half-square-triangle units. Square up each unit to measure 2½" x 2½"

Make 320.

2. Sew together a print and a tan 1½" x 2½" rectangle. Make 320 side units, keeping units together in groups of four matching units. Press the seam allowances toward the print rectangles.

Make 320.

3. Randomly select four half-square-triangle units from step 1. Lay out the half-square-triangle units, four matching units from step 2, and one print 2½" square in three rows as shown. Sew the pieces together in rows, and then sew the rows together. Press the seam allowances in the directions indicated. Make 80 blocks.

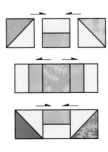 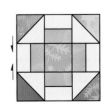

Make 80.

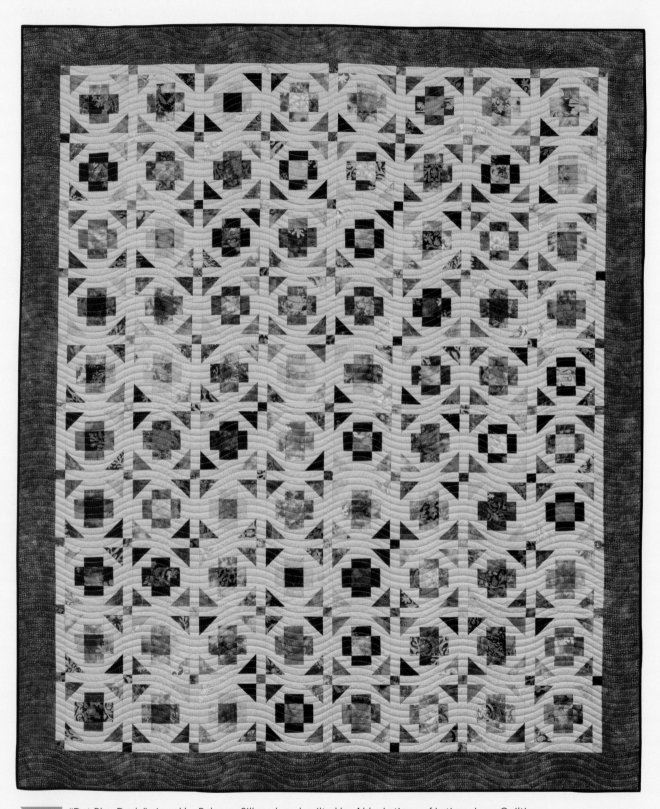

"Dot Plus Dash," pieced by Rebecca Silbaugh and quilted by Abby Latimer of Latimer Lane Quilting
Finished quilt: 65½" x 79½"
Finished block: 6" x 6"

Scale of Prints

You certainly want a variety of fabrics within a scrap quilt, but it's important to keep the scale of prints in line with the proportions of the quilt pieces. This allows the prints to be effective. If you cut an extra-large floral print into 1" finished squares, you'll completely lose the fabric design and it can distort the look of the quilt. Rather than looking like you used one fabric in a specific area, it could look like you raided your stash and threw in whatever you could grab.

The opposite is true, too. Using tiny prints in large pieces isn't all that effective either. Prints that are too small can make a quilt look unfinished. However, small prints can make a great background. Just make sure the print is subtle and doesn't distract from the overall look of the quilt. It's all about balance.

Assembling the Quilt Top

1. Lay out the blocks in 10 rows of eight blocks each, rearranging the colors as needed to create a nice mix. Place tan 1½" x 6½" sashing rectangles between each of the blocks and along the outer blocks. Fill in the open spaces with print 1½" squares.

2. Sew the blocks, sashing rectangles, and squares together in rows as shown in the quilt assembly diagram above right. Press the seam allowances toward the sashing rectangles. Sew the rows together. Press the seam allowances toward the sashing rows.

3. Sew the orange strips together end to end to make a long strip. Measure the length of the quilt top through the middle and near both edges; determine the average of these measurements. From the pieced strip, cut two border strips to the average length. Sew these strips to the sides of the quilt top, matching the ends and easing in any excess. Press the seam allowances toward the border strips.

4. Measure the width of the quilt top through the middle and near both edges; determine the average of these measurements. From the remainder of the pieced strip, cut two strips to the average width. Sew these strips to the top and bottom of the quilt, matching the ends and easing in any excess. Press the seam allowances toward the border strips.

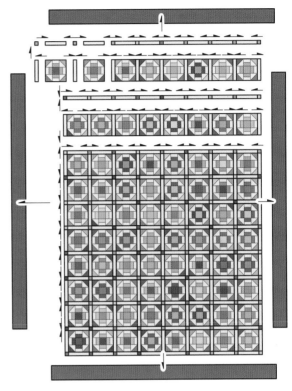

Quilt assembly

Finishing the Quilt

For more information on layering, quilting, or binding, go to ShopMartingale.com/HowtoQuilt and download free illustrated information.

1. Cut and piece the backing fabric so it measures 6" to 8" larger than the quilt top in both directions.

2. Quilt as desired. To play off of the quilt's modern vibe, Abby Latimer quilted wavy horizontal lines that couldn't be more perfect for this design.

3. Use the 2¼"-wide binding strips to bind the quilt.

"Crumpet"
Finished quilt: 24½" x 33¾"

Crumpet

The resurgence of 60° triangles and diamonds in quilts is a look that many quilters—myself included—have grown to love. This quilt pairs both diamonds and triangles in a look that's reminiscent of a traditional quilt, yet is fresh and new with its off-center radiating diamond motif.

Materials

Yardage is based on 42"-wide fabric.

1 Honeycomb OR 40 hexagons of assorted light, medium, and dark prints for blocks*

⅞ yard of light fabric for background

⅓ yard of fabric for binding

1¼ yards of fabric for backing

32" x 41" piece of batting

Template plastic**

60° ruler (optional)**

Each Honeycomb hexagon measures 6" from point to opposite point, and 5¼" from one flat side to the opposite side. Or, use the hexagon pattern on page 59 to cut your own hexagons.

**Template plastic is not required if using a ruler. The 60° ruler needs to have a vertical center line and measurements along the horizontal lines, not side measurements.*

Cutting

From the light fabric, cut:
11 strips, 2¼" x 42"

From the fabric for binding, cut:
4 strips, 2¼" x 42"

Making the Blocks

1. Use the triangle pattern on page 59 to make a template. Use the triangle template (or a 60° ruler) to cut 229 triangles from the light strips. If using a 60° ruler, align the 2¼" line with the edge of the strip.

2. Cut each print hexagon into six triangles as shown.

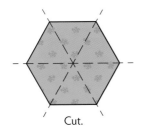

Cut.

3. Use the triangle template to trim the point on each corner of each light and print triangle. Or, you can use a regular ruler to measure 2¼" from each flat side and trim off the point. Removing the points will give you a guide to align the triangles while sewing.

4. Sew light triangles and print triangles together in pairs to make 209 triangle pairs. Press the seam allowances open. Keep the remaining triangles for assembling the quilt top.

SCRAPPY TIP

Less is More

This quilt is the perfect argument for the saying "less is more." This scrappy quilt uses nothing but triangles. Simple! Don't use scrappy quilts as an excuse to throw all caution to the wind; you still need structure in some form to prevent your quilt from looking like a hot mess.

Assembling the Quilt Top

1. Lay out the triangle pairs and the remaining print and light triangles in 19 rows as shown in the quilt assembly diagram on page 58. Each row consists of 11 triangle pairs and either two print triangles or two light triangles as follows:

   Rows 1, 2 ,5, 6, 9, 10, 15, 16, and 19: 11 triangle pairs and two print triangles

   Rows 3, 4, 7, 8, 11, 12, 13, 14, 17, and 18: 11 triangle pairs and two light triangles

   You can discard the remaining 13 print triangles or set them aside for another project.

2. Sew the triangles in each row together, aligning the trimmed points. Press the seam allowances in opposite directions from row to row.

Row assembly

3. Sew the rows together. Press the seam allowances in one direction. Trim the sides of the quilt top all around to square up the corners, making sure to leave ¼" of fabric beyond the last seam intersection for the seam allowance. (Or, you can wait and trim the edges after the quilting is completed.)

Finishing the Quilt

For more information on layering, quilting, or binding, go to ShopMartingale.com/HowtoQuilt and download free illustrated information.

1. Cut and piece the backing fabric so it measures 6" to 8" larger than the quilt top in both directions.

2. Quilt as desired. Small projects can be difficult to quilt due to the bulk of the seams in proportion to the size of the quilt. I quilted simple straight lines to emphasize the diamond pattern. I also densely quilted the light fabric with radiating lines to enhance the design.

3. Use the 2¼"-wide binding strips to bind the quilt.

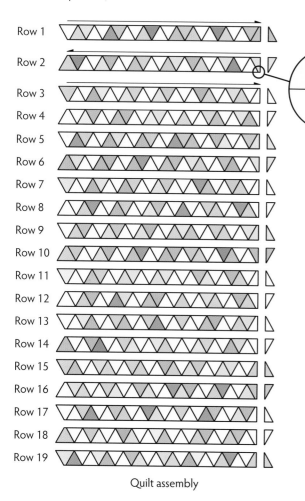

Quilt assembly

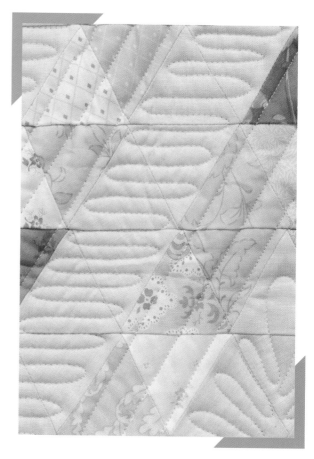

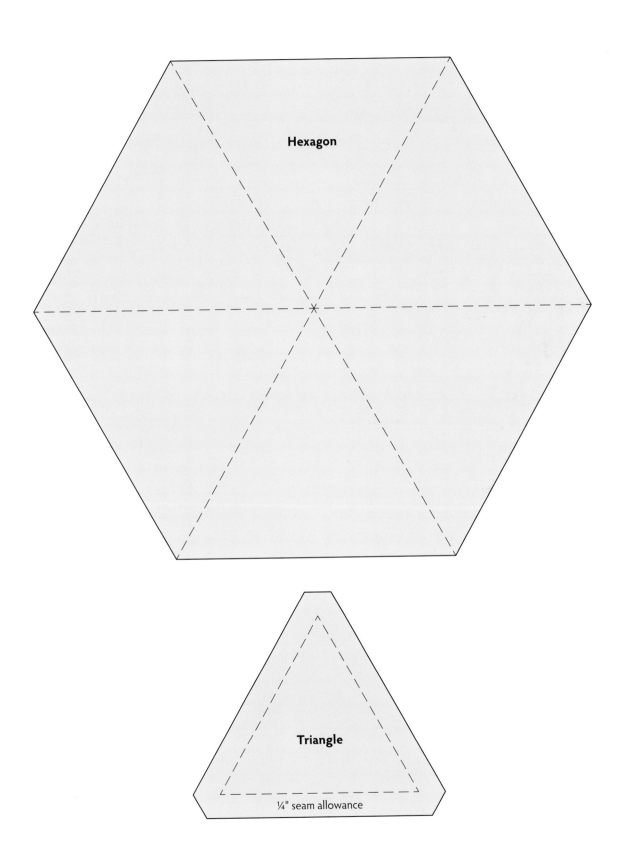

Hexagon

Triangle

¼" seam allowance

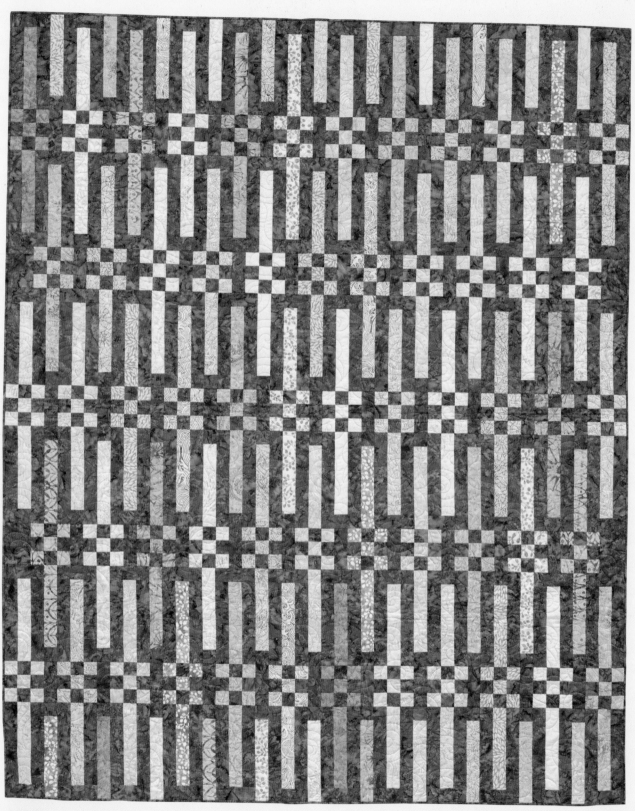

"Patch Stack"
Finished quilt: 71" x 86"
Finished blocks: Nine Patch blocks: 4½" x 4½"
Strip blocks: 4½" x 10½"

Patch Stack

Originally, my plan was to have the blocks in this quilt run horizontally, but once I did the math, it made more sense for them to run vertically. Regardless of the block orientation, this would make a great quilt for a special guy. I made mine in shades of blues and greens to use in our home by the lake. What colors are you imagining?

Materials

Yardage is based on 42"-wide fabric.

3¾ yards of blue batik for blocks

1 Tonga Treats 6-Pack *OR* 20 strips, 6" x 42", of assorted light batiks for blocks

⅔ yard of fabric for binding

5¼ yards of fabric for backing

79" x 94" piece of batting

Cutting

From the blue batik, cut:
   7 strips, 5" x 42"; crosscut into:
     125 rectangles, 2" x 5"
     4 rectangles, 3½" x 5"
   41 strips, 2" x 42"; crosscut into:
     144 rectangles, 2" x 9½"
     298 squares, 2" x 2"

From the assorted light batiks, cut:
   58 strips, 2" x 42"; crosscut *each* strip into:
     3 rectangles, 2" x 9½" (174 total; you'll have 36 extra)
     5 squares, 2" x 2" (290 total)

From the fabric for binding, cut:
   9 strips, 2¼" x 42"

Making the Blocks

1. Lay out five matching light 2" squares and four blue 2" squares in a nine patch setting. Sew the squares together in rows. Press the seam allowances toward the blue squares. Sew the rows together. Press the seam allowances toward the center. Make 58 Nine Patch blocks.

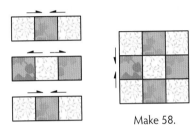

Make 58.

2. Randomly select 36 Nine Patch blocks from step 1 and two light 2" x 9½" rectangles that match each Nine Patch block. Sew blue 2" x 9½" rectangles to both long sides of a light rectangle as shown. Press the seam allowances toward the blue rectangles. Sew a blue 2" x 5" rectangle to one end of each strip unit to make a Strip block. Press the seam allowances toward the blue rectangle. Make two Strip blocks to match each Nine Patch (72 total). Sort the blocks into 36 sets of one Nine Patch and two Strip blocks, all matching.

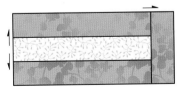

Make 72.

3. For the 22 remaining Nine Patch blocks, select two light 2" x 9½" rectangles that match each block. Sew a blue 2" square to one end of each rectangle to make a pieced strip. Press the seam allowances toward the blue square. Sort the pieces into 22 sets of one Nine Patch block and two pieced strips, all matching.

4. Sew a blue 2" square to one end of each remaining light 2" x 9½" rectangle to make 22 pieced strips. Press the seam allowances toward the blue square.

Make 22.

Assembling the Quilt Top

Refer to the photo on page 60 and the quilt assembly diagram on page 63 for placement guidance throughout.

1. Randomly select 12 of the Nine Patch blocks from step 2 of "Making the Blocks" on page 61 for row 2 and arrange them on a design wall or the floor, leaving 2" between the blocks. Place a blue 2" x 5" rectangle between each block. Place matching Strip blocks above and below each Nine Patch block for rows 1 and 3, as shown in the quilt assembly diagram.

2. For row 4, randomly select 11 of the Nine Patch blocks from step 3 of "Making the Blocks" and place them on the design wall. Center the blocks below the space between the Strip blocks in row 3. Place a blue 3½" x 5" rectangle on each end of the row and place blue 2" x 5" rectangles between the Nine Patch blocks. Then place pieced strips that match the Nine Patch blocks between the Strip blocks in row 3 and below the Nine Patch blocks in row 5.

3. Repeat step 1 for rows 6 and 10, and step 2 for row 8. Use the 22 pieced strips from step 4 of "Making the Blocks" to fill in the spaces in rows 1 and 11.

4. Sew the pieces together into rows. Press the seam allowances toward the blue rectangles. Sew the rows together and press the seam allowances toward the rows of Nine Patch blocks.

Finishing the Quilt

For more information on layering, quilting, or binding, go to ShopMartingale.com/HowtoQuilt and download free illustrated information.

1. Cut and piece the backing fabric so it measures 6" to 8" larger than the quilt top in both directions.

2. Quilt as desired. To mimic the feeling of water and nature for this quilt, I used an allover, wavelike swirl pattern.

3. Use the 2¼"-wide binding strips to bind the quilt.

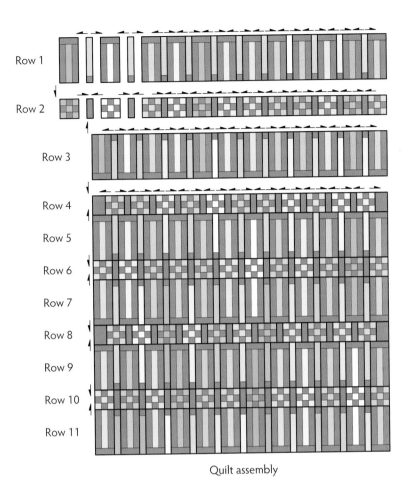

Row 1

Row 2

Row 3

Row 4

Row 5

Row 6

Row 7

Row 8

Row 9

Row 10

Row 11

Quilt assembly

About the Author

Rebecca is a creative soul with a passion for quilting. Thanks to her background in graphic design and her lifelong dabblings in art, Rebecca's interest in all things quilting began with the allure of fabric. After opening Ruby Blue Quilting Studio in 2009, she published her first book, *Seamingly Scrappy* (Martingale, 2013), and continues to create scrappy quilts as often as she can. When Rebecca isn't working on a new quilt at home in Ohio, she's probably traveling with her husband, Ben, discovering a new favorite home away from home. No matter where Rebecca is, you can always find her on her blog at RubyBlueQuilts.blogspot.com.